MANIA KLEPTO

The Book of Eulene

Also by the Same Author

Books of Poetry
Stealing the Children
Premonitions of an Uneasy Guest
Seasons of Mangoes and Brainfire
A Change of Maps

Chapbooks
Returning What We Owed
From a White Woman's Journal
Brief Irreveries
Carolyne Wright: Greatest Hits 1975-2001

Translation
In Order to Talk with the Dead: Selected Poems of Jorge Teillier
(from the Spanish)
The Game in Reverse: Poems by Taslima Nasrin
(from the Bengali)
*Another Spring, Darkness: Collected Poems of Anuradha
Mahapatra* (from the Bengali)
Majestic Nights: Love Poems of Bengali Women

Nonfiction
A Choice of Fidelities: Lectures and Readings from a Writer's Life

MANIA KLEPTO

The Book of Eulene

As told to Carolyne Wright

Author Photo: Elizabeth Samson, Lynchburg College

Cover Art: Eugenia Toledo, "Eulene Pajarística," mixed media collage and
    image from Alicia Caudle of Altered Bits, 2010.

Cover & Book Design: Christine Holbert

FIRST EDITION

ISBN: 9781936370412
LCCN: 2011932324

For Jim (a.k.a. Eulene's Al Terego)

For Jane,
Poetry Sisteh! May
you enjoy these
"stormy syllables" & all
the stories behind them!

Abrazos,
[signature]
Seattle 2011

TABLE OF CONTENTS

I Eulene

II Woman, Money, Watch, Gun

III. Eulene Goes Back to Godhead

I

EULENE

EULENE

I have to give up coffee.
Eulene tosses and turns all night
and I get up in the morning
black and blue and twisted.

My dreams give me a cramp in the throat
when I try to laugh.
Eulene

is the blank-faced onlooker
in all those dreams.
The only thing she will say to me is
"Don't give me away."

Every time I try to sketch Eulene
she slides behind my back.
I can't stop her hands
from reaching around to pick
at the hairs on my chin.

Sometimes I feel like putting Eulene
in an elevator and pushing
the down button. Let her go
to the sub-basement.
She could make a living there,
putting the lids on dreams.

Then she'd be safe.
My hands have tried to strangle her
too many times in dreams,
but she's always jumped out the window
just in time.

Now that I'm awake,
I ought to finish off this last cup
of coffee, and throw
the dregs in the trash.

Maybe then I could go downstairs
and pull the lids off.

Eulene will never notice.
Not until I shake a bag
of dead birch leaves
on the floor where she throws her fits,
leave her the garbage and the dirty cups,
and go outside for good.

"MANIA KLEPTO"

Eulene never comes to shoplift
but to leave things--
rhinestone butterflies she borrowed
from her mother's casket of vanities;
her father's moldering, Bolshevik cigars;
her brother's manic metronome
that ticks in its box
like the crocodile in Peter Pan.

She has to be discreet and furtive
as a Gideon Bible placement clerk,
dart her hand out when the eyes
in the back of the store detective's
head blink. She places each object
so it says, "I've always been here,"
and blends into the merchandise
like a wallflower.

       Petty generosity
made up the family litany,
dinned so long in her ear
she never could forget it,
even between birthdays.
She's spent years trying
to be normal--a taker of tickets
and free rides, the gifts and creatures
of sucker friends' philanthropy.

       Now
she knows better, the mania so familiar
it's conviction. She goes through the motions
like a master evangelist, breaking

into fertile grounds for quick drops
and quicker getaways, subtle Appleseeder
of an excess of possessions. How else
could anyone receive them?

Eulene no longer questions, merely smiles
at the racks of garments, the thin
bored women who assess them.
She deposits the last tatter
she's smuggled in, calm-faced
and professional as a mannequin.

The dressing room corridor turns
into a Valhalla of mirrors,
and Eulene—Dame Quixote armed only
with a bare, bent hanger—
finally contends with the grim
glass-multiplied reflections.

DREAM TELLER

In Eulene's dreams there's a teller
in a barred window who tallies the figures
and sends back the statement
in the morning. He knows Eulene
too well, knows how she fudges
on the balance. He's laid it on the line
too many times for her to mislay
what he means, but still the dreams
don't come out even.

Instead, they balk, back up,
and get stuck in sleep's keyhole
like ransom notes. Eulene's
always missed the rented angels
standing at attention in them,
big and beef-faced as policemen.
She thinks they're sales clerks,
smiles pulling their mouths wide
as toads', pointing with sticky prehensiles
to the One Thing She Really Wants.
But she can't see around them,
see the other sides blinking
like Christmas pendants in the turning light.
She lets herself be gulled so well
she never knows. And they never tell.

When she wakes up, there's no
one to get even with.
Just a red light flashing on and off and on
above the teller's booth.
Outside, the morning drives away
on its official round.

Eulene's left standing there,
crumpled stubs of her canceled passbook
clutched tight in her hand.

EULENE, AGE 12, CURSES THE STATE FAIR

I hate Puyallup,
Eulene thought, lying on the blanket,
fireflies gaudy beyond the screened porch—
lights like candles on a birthday cake,
an eyeful of flowers. September
of her thirteenth year.

          At Puyallup
there were carnival swirls, yellow
and green spokes of the Ferris wheel,
cotton candy on parade like ratted hairdos
bobbing down high school halls.

There were livestock pens: heifers
stamping in piss-sodden straw
that steamed in the hogback sun;
dairy bulls lowering their polled horns,
their pendulous balls swinging
like grenades in ski-mask slings.

There were roving wolf-packs
of teenage boys, jangling
the family heirlooms in their denims,
bellowing down cedar-chip corridors
between the stalls.
In their X'ed-out dreams, Eulene sprung time
with her teeth for them, wind
whipping off her clothes
and they were gone . . .

Eulene: no child by then, and already
everybody's fool.

Her only words were *Don't! Don't!*
Don't! Don't!

But in her head
the loins' masturbatory chant took up
Add more Add more Add more then
throw it all away.
It was the body
of course, saying, *"Up, down, in, out . . .*
A sexual thing, but look at me as whole!"

Eulene looked, all right.
In the sideshow tents: the tarot pack
and the *faux* gypsy seeking dollars
who read her heart in green.
She told Eulene a future of excesses,
golden winks and fingers, the Chinese
cookie's hold on the fortune
of whatever stranger
Eulene made up her mind to want.

She tuned Eulene's money like a flute
and Eulene learned to take what she could get.
Bargain basement affairs—grainy,
low-budget cruelties that toyed with her
before she woke up to the world.

When Eulene got home, there was a book
of consolation prizes waiting for her,
already overdue. And her cousins
from Humptulips, their freeloader
faces intent on their food.
A studied grouping: plates passed around
as in an early Van Gogh low life.

They ignored Eulene. *"More pie!"*
they demanded. *"Slam the potatoes."*

In her worst flash-forwards
what could Eulene keep
of all these subterfuges?
Already she knew the waterfall
and coffee filter would not save her,
and through the ersatz looking glass
she could glimpse darkly
only the face of her own intentions
gone astray.

Nothing from these last few weeks of childhood
when progesterone was rampant
and all there was in the salvific skies
was rain.

for Deborah Woodard

ON VACATION WITH EULENE

"dos puertas que al viento van y vienen
sombra   a   sombra"

—César Vallejo, *Trilce*

Overweighted we've come, under the fog,
taking on a North Atlantic wind
long after the others fall asleep.
I shiver and decode Vallejo
while Eulene hunches into her bad mood
like a turtle's neck.
She plucks out eyelashes

        one

by

    one.

"Why?" I ask, but she keeps
her mouth shut, as usual.

When will she finally shirk
the perfectionist's punishment,
the picking and plucking and push push push,
and look wide open in my eyes?
"That's the road," she says,
and makes detour after detour
of excuses not to.
It's the terrible joy of swerving
that makes Eulene grab at the wheel.

"Let go," I tell myself
when Eulene takes off with her weight

10

and the counterfeiting of her smile.
"If she walks out without her slicker on,
the *Gesundheitgeist* that grabs at her
won't snare your breath.
Her clockwork God ticks off
each lash that falls. In the morning,
He'll burn off her fog."

All's well, the nucleic code
throbs under all denials.

EULENE'S BROKEN LIFELINE

*"If the fool would persist in his folly
he would become wise."*

—William Blake

Years ago, the fortune-teller scowled
at Eulene's broken lifeline.
Eulene laughed, later, back in her room
with her jogging shoes
and Type-A lighting, her books
Creative Rage and *How to Prioritize
Your Options.*

                She knew all about
the body's planetary pull,
how the population bomb
and landfills of garbage on the fault lines,
the I-beam weight of cities,
had thrown the crabbed old zodiacs
out of kilter, and no one but she
was in charge here. Her own *guru*
and *comandante,* with the Power
of Plus-Charge Thinking.

                What else
was there to go for?
She was climbing the corporate
totem pole, one wolf-mask
at a time. She still believed
in potlatch over scalp, hand
over fist: taking things slowly,
proceeding with a woman driver's caution

where the pay-scale needle
hovered for years on Hazardous.
She believed in interest rates
and the cost-of-living index.
She made down payments
on everything in sight.

• • •

Then her broker ran off
with her analyst, like the dish
with the spoon. Her horoscope
was filled with I-told-you-so's
and volcanoes erupting on the dark side
of the moon. The spider threads of her safety net
gave way, and Eulene sat down hard
in the epicenter of her cluttered life,
trying to explain the confusion.

She'd used the circus-seal method
of balancing her budget. Worn T-shirts
that said *I Don't Get Mad
I Get Even.* Loved only men
with dark hair and green cards
and one-way tickets to the edges of the earth
where *Drop Off* was a command
not a caution sign. She'd sown nothing
but downfall-teeth all along.

• • •

Now she sits in the ancient history
museum café on no-admission-charge afternoons,
eating melon balls and goat cheese
off other visitors' abandoned plates.
In the free brochures, she reads up

on see-through pleats from Cheops
to the Ptolemys. Her own clothes
quiescent for a change, with their lived-in
died-in look.

                    But she's not complaining.
She's still at the receiving end
of a long dynasty of hand-me-downs.
She has her youth, her health,
her weight on the Chase Manhattan scale
still lower than her IQ. She has
her wide-open calendar, and a dial tone
in which anything could happen.

                    • • •

She's planning her comeback
like a facial make-over,
a before-and-after inside job.
As if all the king's scarab's
and all the king's *kaas*
could cast their jackal-headed spells
and slap her back together

once she's cracked along her plate lines
like a tectonic egg. She ignores
the warning in the center of her palm
which flashes its *memento mori* at her
like a small-town traffic light
at 3 a.m.: faithfully and for no one.

Poor forked fool, Eulene,
persisting in her folly as if wisdom
will trickle down someday like the rain
or a supply-side theory into her brain.

CONJURE EULENE

A borrowed thought drifts through her sleep.
Its neglected owner wants her
to return it, sends her overdue slips,
threatens to let her synapses
go out of print. She wakes to find her hands
scribbling illegible replies on IOU slips
no believable characters
could get away with. The next reply
will write itself, dispense with hands
altogether.

Where will Eulene fit?
The thought expands, she shrinks,
a jot shaken from a fountain pen
onto the blank plain of the page.
She can't see how far away
the margins of books have moved,
blue as the elbows of rivers.

That's when the thought
takes after her, starving for attention,
a fugitive of leash laws.
She can't keep it at memory's length.
It clambers up the steep banks
of the paragraphs, its jaws dead-set.

Soon
the thought will wake Eulene
in the odd hours, spread remaindered
fingers at the moon, dangle
its Damoclean handcuffs.

The crack in her forehead will widen
to an eye, and stare straight out
at eternity, in wonder.

EULENE'S HALLOWE'EN

Eulene's a shunpiker,
but her lovely meanders
get less lovely farther down
the road, and the toll's inflation's
geometric on each deviant inch.

Take Hallowe'en as a for-instance.
All the death-wish heads
were glued like flies to the wallpaper,
and Eulene, got up in *sari*
and clown white, glided to the graveyard
with her household's other wraiths.
What could she do there
but play tombstone leapfrog
and listen to midnight's pumpkin shrieks?
Her obeisance with folded hands
was a posture for no friends,
and her best pal Salvatore
wore Osh-Kosh coveralls, hillbilly slouch,
and belch. They'd never match.
At home, one plain, non-Jack-o-Lantern candle
spilled twelve threads of wax. It was time
to get off the boneyard's muddy tracks.
But Salvatore had disappeared
with a carbon-compound wizard
and a wraith.

                    Give up that apple-bob,
Eulene. Even in mask and costume
you walk home alone.

AFTER HARVARD SQUARE:
EULENE'S BREAD AND CIRCUSES

What a smattering of culture
Eulene's got. A chopstick here,
a tatter of Punjabi cotton there,
and on her walls, the latest
in the Vorpal Gallery's catalogue.
Conducing, all of it, to what?
Not to the overpopulation of the heart,
or to the string-twangings
of the popular affectioners.
Not, surely, to *Gimme lo-ove, LOVE!*

No. Eulene stalks down the street,
her eyes burning the whole show
thin, her mind's hands knocking out
the flim-flam frames that prettify
life's knuckled force.
Sometimes she strays,
ghosting past the showrooms
where they plug salvation into stereos . . .

Until she remembers the bare
walls of early summer: sea
wind through an open door,
and salt-water light splashing
on patio flagstones, the swept floor.

EULENE'S LETTING SALVATORE GO,

dropping the ropes off.
After all, he never was a grand piano
or a safe being lowered
from the thirty-seventh floor.
Just a boy trying to be holy
without the seamless tunic or the wings,
making everyone else's aureole
go dim. He had to be the saint
with the most gold leafing in the room.
Eulene was spoiling him,
patting his curly head and taking his arm
as if they really were as warm
as friends. "But it's cold
the flyway that I'm on,
and I'm going north this fall,"
he said. That's why he won't relent
under affection, but looks straight on,
a stern V of eyebrows.

Eulene knows now
that love's more than a tail
hypnotized with salt, or a fig leaf
and pectorals on a pedestal,
or even the glow that lets her see
the angels' wings. Love's driving her
to robes and rosaries and the blood
that pulses through that glow.

Salvatore knows. That's why
he turns his head away,
why no doves teeter on the stem

behind his eyes. Besides,
he'd never let himself fall low enough
to kneel beside her where she prays.

EULENE'S A NUN NOW,

kneeling in her college room.
No vows yet, and no vestments,
she dares to call the winter sun
down on her house. Let it sear away
the hashish smells, dog stains
in the hallway. That bummer,
memory, building its nests in the drawers.
Let it burn into the beer-bleared eyes
averted when Eulene walks in.
Fears that roll the sleeping bags tighter
behind Venetian blinds. Bullies
who look for victims in the mirrors.

Eulene packs her only change
of clothes, peels the labels
from her judgment jars,
the fist in her rib cage
clenching and unclenching.
She's signed her soul up
for a job, reassigned all wakeful
questionings, quick-change artists
moving in next door. She holds
her bones to their own promises,
escape routes into the country
cordonned off.

EULENE'S *NOCHE OSCURA*

When Eulene walked in, habits
turned the color of strangle-vines.
Nuns scrubbed the chapel
on their knees, the wrathful afternoon
glowering through stained glass,
choir stalls halved by Manichaean shadow.

                                    Now,
Eulene sneaks out during Evening Prayer
to work on her icon of Big Nun—
fishwife in a chain-gang rosary
and goat's-hair veil, her Popeye forearms
tattooed with the Pontiff's face.

Eulene hums snatches of the Vatican Rag
and the house gets narrower.

Who else would laugh
at the prioress's black tabby
with white paws and monsignor collar,
or christen it *Magnificat*
at the vestry water cooler?
All night it yowls from the dead hemlock
in the convent close, Eulene's
cri-de-coeur's semblable.

What is she after?
She's weary of tinsel stars,
names in neon aureoles
breakdancing on the big marquees.
Through "Religious Preference"

she still draws a line
straight as a brain-scan.

In Sunday School
she learned Sign of the Cross
as Theatre. Later, she wore earplugs
against the sound of one hand clapping,
deprogrammers her parents hired
hot on her trail.

                    These days,
she answers their calls
in Dracula's Daughter's voice:
*"Sacre Bleu Convent,
Stigmata Vile You Vait."*

She's good at shrinking herself
to fit disappointment. When she hears
the prioress's boots on the stairs
she dumps her crayons in the potted plants,
drops Big Nun into the frame
behind the Founding Mother's portrait.

She stands up to collect her dogface.
When she looks down, a stranger's shadow
glides from underneath her shoes.

II

WOMAN, MONEY, WATCH, GUN

EULENE ENTERS THE ME GENERATION

Any day now, Eulene
could fly in from the Antilles
with a prime-time script
scribbled on hotel stationery,
her briefcase crammed with towels
from the Granada Hilton—
everything she needed to make it
through the revolution.

                    This time
Eulene knows her place
in the infrastructure. She can quote you
her 18-carat chances,
a model of the Walk-Thru Woman
on her desk. She'll play her cards,
answer the telephone in five
different voices, a new account
on each line demanding the latest
figures in gunboat stock. Who else
would pay her way?

Not the baby-food conglomerates,
their blond formula-packet infants
voted most popular in the Third World.
Not the postcard people, the suntan
connoisseurs. Not the Who's Who
in hot tubs. They all know
the future's in microchips
and mail-order weapons.

                    For years
Eulene's tidied up after

other people's bad trips,
given in to every primal scream.
Not any more.
It's a tough world
and she's left her heart
in escrow long enough.

Eulene's going to step into
the cash flow, rake it in
at last. Between lovers, she'll play
Dungeons and Dragons with all
the stock she's taken in America.
She'll switch on the six o'clock
body count. Pay the piper
out of some other worst-case scene-
stealer's Book of Dreams.

THE MORNING MAIL:
EULENE'S BRIEF IRREVERIE

She gets invitations—form letters
with her name filled in
from mail-order guest lists.
She reads them at bulk rate
before the trash can closes
her subscription. She riffles through
the well-digested readers, the endless
once-a-lifetime offers,
the self-thumping Bible kits,
to set straight the states
and kingdoms she's seceded from.

Eulene's reached her liable limit.
She's run too many business rounds,
scratching tasks off lists
like lice off a rabbit.

Meanwhile, a surveilling eye
on a retractable stalk peers at her
from all directions.
It's taking notes.
Digits click off behind its retina
like gambling slots. Satisfied,
it pulls back to its box
and snaps the lid down.

                    Eulene gets up,
knocks the egg shells from her plate,
and waits—not for the clock
to bong out doom, nor for her ride,
its ancient Goodyears rubbing white caulk

on the curb—but for the eyes
that glare from the papering
as she leaves the room.

"What have I done," she asks,
"to earn such coverage?
What Cerberus lurks at my gates,
a dog in postman's clothing?
Could I sneak by, just once,
all watchers but the single Eye: I,
a refugee of blindfolds
in a world at large?"

EULENE LEAVES THE ANCESTRAL
MANSION (FOR GOOD)

The sea squid on the hat rack
wriggles its tentacles in her face.
She can't hang up her sou'wester
without being wrapped
in an eight-armed embrace.
But Eulene forgives: its writhing's
calisthenic, and it, too, poor hanger-on,
flounders out of place here.

It's the knick-knack shelves
she must avoid, the fusty old victrolas,
lace antimacassars jostling
each other for the parlor air.
It's underwater-thick with dust
in here, and a fly that gave up
on the glass pane long ago
drones dully.

                    If Eulene thought,
"All this house needs
is a mummy
that falls from the closet
like a fold-out ironing board,"
her folks would get it,
putting two more revolutions
in their circular account.

But she waives her power of suggestion
for a stronger cure. Three dawns
a week, she ducks the long reek
hanging in middle air—the ghost

of a cigar—and hands-and-knees it
out the grillework door.

The tentacles fall off her then
like tarred rope from a mooring,
and she picks up her life again--
breath's prodigal daughter making her allotted
progress, hungry for the sun's
refractions through the glass,
those auroral spectra that fan out
along the far shores of her childhood
like a promise almost forgotten.

CRITICAL THEORY: EULENE

(Instructions to Her Double)

Never bring your elbows to this class.
There's barely room to duck the dean's eye,
scowls of the harpies at the front desk, thesis
committee's derision coming at you
like a clammy fun-house hand.

Eulene wakes at dawn, love nailed
high on her list of intentions.
She reminds herself to hold her hormones'
bayings in abeyance till the right bells
ring, get to class on time.

This time, she learns how to manipulate
the inside views: words that have heard
of each other, ridden up elevators
together, never yet been introduced. Eulene
tries to remember what comes after

How Are You? But it's a damp fuse,
and the omniscient author's prose
monotonous as the barroom conquests
in the late late shows.

You doze.
Lovers drift side by side in your thoughts
like leaves on a river. You peel off
superlatives like clothes, the dream
stands up to repeated readings,
there's not one adjective to edit. . . .

. . . Eulene starts: it's over. The class falls out
like a regiment–the same show of feet,
meters winding down in all the faces,
briefcases tight with thoughts too stuffy
to admit they've met. Left out,

like a student from one of those small,
angry countries, Eulene sees her best harangues
have dwindled, sunk to footnotes [1]
in some rival text. Even Eulene's
old lovers, whose best moans

quote hers,[2] keep the credit.
A secret zero starts its slow
growth in her heart.
It will look for allies everywhere.

1. See #1 above!
2. "Oh! Oh!"

SUCCESS BOMB #45

She stared at ruin. Ruin stared straight back.

Divested of her armor of thrift-store duds
Eulene's the success bomb, striking minor
triumphs, like enemies, off her hit list.
Lounging in the bathtub's bubbly suds
for hours, she plays "Start Me Up" on her
CD player a hundred times till her best

bodacious parts are wrinkly as gin-
stewed prunes. "What, we hurry?" Eulene
growls, between the subwoofer's thudding booms
and the rhetorical popping of bonbons
into her lip-glossed kisser. *"Ah!"* she moans,
and palms, like an oracle, the H_2O stains

blessing her e-book of Berryman's *Dream Songs*—whichever
18 lines of frantic jabber her finger
lands on: her next career move! Then: *Horrors!*
The e-book slips from her grasp, disappears
sub-bubblewards. Electrifying revelation!
Eulene's last flash as the jobless dark comes un-

POSTMORTEM: EULENE

Occluded stars bully me
like ghosts among twilit half domes.
They mock my tongue
with honey and silver, blood-
hued moons and tree sloths
that unwrap their slow shovels

and plummet past the lustre palms
in a mottled swoon. Their tails
never did curl properly. So
what about the blood count
of the stars, the night's relentless weather?

Cancún couldn't let on about its revelers
under such yield signs, hedged about
with corduroy and sticky milk.
The scatter-bird snaps the quetzal's
neck and panthers grind their incisors.
Only names whose conjure fires

ash out a superhuman scorn
jump ship and disappear into the port's
labyrinth of alleys. New lovers move
to safe houses after curfew
and emerge next season

with land-legged suits, new pin codes
in their documents, new histories—
they've always been here.
Charismatic black sheep, the baby
in the brain cries Baby, its mother
opens her blouse in the Swiss-cheese

riddle of hymnals. Jezebel is the name tag
on the morgue's latest arrival. So
why don't I turn my face, rueful
blue but featureless, toward
the self-effacing cradle?

EULENE JUDGES THE SUITORS: A DREAM

In the high maritime swells
they come lurching in by twos.
More like a diluvian menagerie
about to founder on Ararat
than men. The chaperones
loll in flamingo *chaise longues*
sipping gin and tonics. Eulene
lingers near her parents
in their love-it or leave-it
receiving line.

Her father has some gripe
against each prospect in the *grand salon*.
One is pimply and introverted;
he's spent the last two fiscal cycles
uprooting bindweed from a P-patch
in Toledo. Another sits in full lotus
in the porthole bay, condensation
droplets on his frozen daiquiri
his only liquid assets, a runner-up
from too crepuscular a product line.
The last one her father glares at
is bumming cigarettes from the *chaise longues.*

Eulene's mother arranges her face,
her grin quick-frozen, hairspray
which lacquers her blonde bouffant
enlarging the holes in the ozone layer.
The mood in the room depends
upon the vertical challenge of her glances.

Eulene squats on the parquet floor
to pull at the run in her stocking.
She knows she's on the *Starboard Out Port Home*
list—her deck stacked with excess cargo
and always on the wrong side of the climate.
The party spins off like a waltzing class
and Eulene stares at vortices of drain water
turning back on themselves
as the cruise ship crosses the equator . . .

. . . and Eulene sits up as the parquet floor
resolves into a counterpane
in the tartan patchwork of her lineage.
Her standards poor, her prospects
plummeting like nuclear plant futures
after Chernobyl, she wakes up
to the coffee's foresworn smell
and wonders who exactly is to blame.

EULENE DRESSES A SQUID

*When you have successfully prepared the recipes
on this poster, send in for your "Certificate
of Accomplishment" as recognition of your interest
in America's underutilized species.*

—National Marine Fisheries Service

(Provincetown, Cape Cod)

1.
Dear Sirs:
I have prepared squid
six different ways. Please send me
my Certificate, officially justifying
my expertise:

                      I started with confidence
and visions of a species
gradually shedding its confusion.
A cartoon squid in a chef's cap
pointing at loins and flanks and chops
his cousin on the wall chart
had been subdivided into: *Historia Animalium*
circa 1959, a *Reader's Digest* version
of Order Out of Chaos
and Understand Your World.

A smaller knife would have helped,
vanadium steel scaled down
to the chitin, cuttlebone
that knocked against pilings
in every dream.

But ink
clouded my intentions—
a smokescreen to unmap the clues,
cumulus with a storm
for lining, the squid's whereabouts
camouflaged by the shape
of other creature's weather.

Tentacles presented their own problems,
grappling with the cutlery
as if ungrateful. The blade poised,
uncertain what it wanted.

I made the first cut
like a fair dealer. The viscera
bloomed from its head-footed
tangle: kelp's Magellanic clouds
in an underswell where the first strike
must always be the deepest.

2.
After that, silence weighed anchor
in my thoughts. I made my peace
with chitin and beak and bleared,
accusatory eye-stalks. I cast off
the rest—desires propelling themselves
backwards through the forgotten shoals
of dream . . .

Gentlemen,
I submit to you this voucher.
As I write, purple stains on my fingers
push up like pucker kisses. My eyes
blur, I push back from my work,

my past some principle of order
solving nothing.

              Keep your Certificate.
I am the sea's ink-mantled daughter,
moving toward deeper water.
My eyes, transparent, have always
agreed with their surroundings.

EULENE STAYS THE COURSE

Not yet wise to the disaster
imperative, Eulene teaches her eyes
to blur for self-protection. No visions
no regrets. Always at the cable station
some worst-case scenario scrolls
out of the control-room fax machine,
defying all final solutions.
Meanwhile, out in the Real World
Eulene keeps on overdoing it,
jostling through the rush-hour
subway tunnels of the baby boom,

a salmon to spawning. Each year
she adds a whole page to her *résumé,*
waits her turn on the search
committee's fish ladder.
She eyes the other candidates'
briefcases and prep-school scarves
in the ice-cream parlor waiting room.
She can finger her take-a-number
as anxiously as the best of them,
watch the forward march
of digits on the wall counter

like the Dow Jones closing average.
In these inflationary times
even Eulene's stocks are on the rise.
But she's not taking any chances.
She's put away her love beads,
signed up for courses in computer
programming and lowered expectations.
She knows the Big Boys

watch her glance from right to left
before punching in, her party membership
obvious as *cholo*-writing

on the housing project walls.
They've got a whole microchip
on her at the National Bank
of Intrigue, and they're not afraid
to deploy it. Eighty million more
where she came from. Survival's
the name of the game for the rat
bulge in the gopher snake.
Why didn't Eulene's parents think
of this before they filled up
America with subdivisions?

WOMAN, MONEY, WATCH, GUN

Eulene's lover wakes with a start.
Something missing: woman,
money, watch, gun.
His life deciduous as October
at the business end of a pawn ticket.
He's always been embarrassed
by crosshairs and calibers
and the biggest hits by the Sex Pistols.
"Step on Your Watch" the last song
before the radio signed off.
His watch bleated every hour.
There was a tiny sheep inside,
white-faced and digital. He counted
on its liquid-crystal half-life.

Lately he's been entering
all the contests: the cereal box-top
sweepstakes, the weekend jackpot
in lotto. He clips
the two-for-one coupons.
Eulene tells him, "It takes money
to make money." That's easy
for her to say, when half America
is living in its cars,
and he has hundreds of memories
of motels. He knows the IRS
is opening his mail, while he roots
in the coin returns of pay phones.

Eulene? He'll never get rid of her.
She's with him like facial scars
or DDT in his genes.

Even if he begged her to stay,
she'd see through him and do it.
Her name clings to everything
he thought was his. No one
should be as sure as she is
of what she wants: a gun, a watch,
a belt full of money,
the perfectly made-up face
of the woman who goes through
his pockets in his dreams.

AN ORDINARY EVENING IN
NEW ORLEANS—EULENE'S SIGNIFICANT
OTHER SPEAKS

Insomnia struck again, so Eulene and I
transplanted all the plants.
The Norfolk Pines in their nitrogen-
poor soil, their fronds nodding
like art-deco fans. The wandering Jew
named after a recent winner
of the Pulitzer. Cacti that spilled
from the mantle, all tentacles,
a sideshow of dire warnings.

Why fight it, we told ourselves.
Death's countdown is closer every minute.
We plugged up the roots
with chalky green pastilles,
their 6-3-1-3 formulae
like Jack-and-the-Beanstalk cure-alls.

All the greenhouse gauges' needles
nosed toward success. Even the Aspidistra
that wilted every winter under its gro-light,
sicklied o'er with the pale cast
of rot, began to sit up and take notice.

Then we cracked open a six-pack
of generic beer, and turned on the VCR
to watch a bootleg copy of *The Rose*.
Eulene thought she was in for two hours
of some long-stemmed symbol of perfection,
not her own fright-wigged look-alike

bumping and grinding to an eleventh-hour beat
between the stage door and the morgue.

But then the phone rang: some crackpot
ranting about briefcases full of pipe bombs
in the baggage claims. I got on the line
with my best precinct commander's voice.
The moon came up, and in the yard
the *mantra* bird had all the answers,
chanting *"Gurdjieff! Gurdjieff!"*
from the crepe myrtle.

                    The couple next door
was at it again, turning Mahler's Third
up all the way, slamming the *Britannica's*
bookshelves to the floor. So much
for the discreet charms of the bourgeoisie.

We switched to TV.
The guest on the Tonite Show
whistled "Chattanooga Choo-Choo"
through his teeth.

                    Eulene stomped out
to throw cold water on her efforts—
all the transplants had keeled over
like deportees in freight cars,
little green *refuseniks.*
Eulene let out her Medusa yell,
tore into the cactus like a nest of copperheads,
buried the shovel to the hilt
in Vigoro. A clay pot
shattered on the shed wall.

What could I do
but head off to the den, tune in
the shortwave: container ships
anchored far out in the Gulf.
All this education, I thought,
and where has it gotten us?
Might as well be Dar es Salaam

as Dixie; and we, Berlitz travelers
trying to fast-forward the learn-
while-you-sleep cassettes,
with presidents in the gun sights
of lone killers: towns where the secret
service chief hands out silver bullets,
and there's never been a conspiracy, ever.

"&"

The Goddess of the Ampersand
  Eulene
  strolls across the browned-out golf

course lawn, fingering her love beads.
  She's just pulled another all-nite shape-
  shift: star barista at the nearby cyber-punk

café, & she's taking the short cut home, skirting
  the gassed-up guzzlers' golf carts
  & shaking her mane at their *Keep Out* —

Trespassers Will Be Fed to Lions
  signs. They've got no stomach for their threats
  but what about her own empty semiotics?

Dawn time is the right time,
  she croons to herself,
  to make lists of her failings—

too many pearls in her birth sign,
  her add-a-planet zodiac
  rolling over the parts of speech,

the periodic elements of her landscaping.
  Who, in her antic pantheon,
  would cut the grass?

She can no longer punctuate
  the weather, parse the clouds, or
  chase *El Niño* from the soggy dunes.

He's always been a bad boy
        & she forgets her connectives, now
        faltering at the edge of the sand trap

like a weather forecaster when the teleprompter
        short-circuits *&* the live-feed
        screen swims with split infinitives.

Eulene stands there slack-jawed: the latest
        of her newly-fangled senior moments
        looms large as a thunder cloud

moving in over the jazz funeral parade
        where she used to second-line
        under a fringed parasol with

her old lover Merlin Diogenes,
        M. D., a.k.a. Mahatma Dog. Who said
        he had a remedy for anything?

He's long since let his sleeves down,
        danced off in his handloomed
        crescent-moon *&* starburst cape,

panting after some teenaged
        Pre-Raphaelite sylph. He left
        Eulene to dangle like a modifier

for someone else's interruptive clause,
        not even her own sentence. But no mind-
        forged manacles for her. Between good grief's

ellipses, Eulene recalls how the *"&"* first
        curled around itself from Carolingian scribes'
        shorthand for *et:* late medieval Latin

and getting short schrift at the stand-up
　　　　scriptorium, but easier to read, post-Gutenberg,
　　　　in some fonts than in others. "&

so what?" thundered Merlin, morphed to
　　　　Michael the auto-redactive archangel
　　　　in Eulene's last argument with him,

flaming stylus like a Fourth of July sparkler
　　　　in his gauntlet, scribbling in darkness
　　　　yet another giga-bit of useless lore.

Brandishing your ampersands again? Eulene
　　　　always wanted to challenge him
　　　　but it would have been no use.

"It's my sign," he told her, it marked him
　　　　one of the hippest of an exclusive coterie
　　　　of outsiders. He'd cornered the market

on the iconography of anomie—it drove
　　　　the booking agents wild. Fans
　　　　queued up, their lines of credit

made for sympathetic mojo
　　　　let the air out of his ambition.
　　　　He never caught on to the irony

but no matter. Eulene was left
　　　　holding his luggage & dousing wand
　　　　like a porter at baggage claim,

knowing the exact same tactics
　　　　never would have worked for her.
　　　　These days, others compete to valet-park

his signifying vehicle, & Eulene
   can fend for herself, thank you.
   Merlin's got no devil-moon magic left

to impose on his last goddess like a palimpsest
   to make her look as if she were alive.
   She's her own moveable type these days

& he can't bar anyone's exit or re-entry
   thru the pearly wisdom teeth
   of Hell-Mouth. Eulene's finally hit

her stride, hit the mind's Delete key
   & poofed him. Still, her charts predict
   she's gonna need her own ampersand

man to fold her stormy syllables in
   like a Monday morning special. Why?
   (Merlin's cryptic persona making a getaway

over the lightning-struck horizon.) Why?
   Because she likes herself. Eulene's
   a gregarious loner, she never

lacks for companions. Her empyrean realms
   shimmer with brilliant losers
   who tuck the conjunct consonants in

before they turn up the gas jets.
   Not this goddess, though. She's always been
   a survivor, stroking her Mardi Gras bead

rosary as a stay against confusion.
   She's gonna go beyond the *fin de siècle*
   fed-up pose, the poseur's over-priced *mantras*

to the real beatitude, even if the mind's walls
      are closing in, the conjunctions come unstrung
      like unspelled pretensions, & Merlin's

still entwined with everything she does
      like a calligraphic lion lifted from minuscule
      & propped up on this greensward,

blocking her path with his efflorescent snarl
      & at the same time
      showing her the way.

III

EULENE GOES BACK TO GODHEAD

PAGAN PANEGYRIC: EULENE

Astrology
beats Christianity.
Crystal balls, Astarte's
diaphanous veil-dance, outstrip
evangelism's empty heft. How so?
First, you high priestesses of cybershopping
get to keep your Maybelline and miniskirts,
hotpants and go-go boots, da-glo posters of Elvis,
Iron Butterfly and Cream, weekends with your
    rockstar studbucket
just back from the Moondog Big Bang Coronation Ball and
Kowabunga Bluesfest, getting it on in his Malibu Beach
    cabaña, with
Lovebeads dripping from bedposts, and lava lamps'
    cherry and erotic butterscotch undulations
moving in mirror-syncopation to your love-thrusts. Who
    could have it better?
No way to beat those odds, or press the juice from
    those sacrimonious grapes
on the Mount of Olives, the Garden of Gethsemane's
    penultimate regrets. Next door to which
Pilate washes his hands in silver fingerbowls and asks
    the Pharisees if there are any further
questions. The graybeards shrug, resume their dovening,
    folding their grievances into
        the oldest human grief. Meanwhile, the
ragged-haired non-union actor drags his plywood cross
    through the studio backlot's Via
        Dolorosa dust like the real
simulacrum. Only groans, no lines hence no residuals for
    this redeemer, though his part's
        the crux and epicenter of

the whole millennial passionfall. Between scenes,
  he smokes in trailer-shade, reads Tarot
    for future gigs. Hanged man and hierophant
unmask his dangerous luck. *Aw, chuck it,* he thinks.
  Make up with Eulene (amateur bellydancer playing
    Magdalene). In her bungalow at
Venice Beach, they used to ball in palm-fringed
  sunlight spilling onto Javanese floormats. Then
    his jug band's touring schedule revved, he
wanted his space, cancelled their romance like maxed-
  out credit cards. Her anguish loomed, Cassandra
    keening over nuclear ruins, until the set of this
X-Files induced fantasy of alien abduction back to
  33 A.D., Magdalene a cyborg who'd washed
    that Son of Man right out of her hair.
You'd think Hollywood would learn—what happened
  in ancient days keeps happening: Magdalene loves
    Jesus; Eulene, Dwayne. At least Jesus
      has a higher calling: the
Zeitgeist on High zaps him from the marriage canopy,
  Eulene sobs tomb-side in her zodiac-print veil.
    Now what? Stay tuned for next week's
      thrilling revelations!

MISS EULENE IN THE VICTORIAN PARLOUR

(York Castle Musuem)

Eulene drifts through the Period Rooms
like a ghost seeking a keeper.

She's lugged a mammoth handbag on this trip,
stitched from the skin of an electric eel
that short-circuited on the ocean floor.

It's her newest acquisition,
end of a generation of plastic sacks
too frail to hold up under the notebooks
books film canisters postcards maps brochures
serviettes saved from coffee shops,
and Saran-wrapped scraps from every meal
since she left the States.

                Someday,
she thinks, *I'll have to travel lighter.*

She confronts at last the genuine
décor of her soul: lion-clawed *chaise longues,*
pearl-handled coal scuttles,
mantel clocks with Doric marble columns
like the Head Offices of Westminster Bank.

All the long-dead denizens.
What more could she ask?
She eavesdrops on guilty laughter,
gasps of recognition
from silver-haired visitors falling
back into their childhoods behind her.

They groan about mauve wallpaper
and windows designed to drive away the light,
how their child-selves struck with ostrich-
feather dusters at Wedgwood and Willow
Ware tea sets, how they crouched
after chores by the fire screen
and patted the ceramic pit bull,
its bark as glazed as its bite.

Now, transfigured only by their generations'
slow dissolve, they edge away from Eulene—
eclipsed in the sycophantic shadows
interrogating her own *fin-de-siècle*
aesthetics: Could she lay doilies
on velvet armrests, and doilies

on top of those doilies? Could she lounge
on velveteen love seats with peacock-
claw feet as their aphrodisiac billows
morph into marital-duty davenports
upholstered with grim gray twill? She admits—
she's nibbled the Prince Albert *petit fours*
and sipped from the laudanum teacups.

                                    Someday,
she thinks, *I'll have to change my strategy.*

 Eulene makes tracks past the Queen
Victoria Longest-Reign-on-Record
plate, the Winston Churchill teapot
with cigar-stump spout,
Blitzkrieg dolls with porcelain scowls
not amused by England's finest hour—

back to her own post-facto generation.
Eulene walks out of Ye Olde Castle Gift Shoppe
stocked with everything for which
she'd never find a use: the Princess Di
blow-dryer, the Andie and Fergie
coffee mugs. She has medium-range plans

to shed the obsessive collector's vestigial
heft, hum *knick-knack, bric-a-brac,*
give a dog a bone, and crawl back
to her hideaway behind a FOR SALE sign
over a boarded-up garage on Swinegate.
No need to wonder when (if ever)
Ms. Eulene goes rolling home.

SPECTRE AND EMANATION AT JFK

Eulene's become a sort of walking
psychic waste dump.
She can't stroll through
the busiest airport in the nation
without drawing the flotsam and jetsam
of half the space-case earth—

panhandlers, suitcase
quick-change artists, muggers
serving their long apprenticeships,
boys just off the boat struggling
with outboard-sized floor polishers
as if adding years to their sentences.

With all the hangers-on these days
doing their hungry bees'-dance toward her,
Eulene has acquired new sympathy
for rotten fruit.

                    She tries to fend off
the young men in red tennis shoes
and saffron robes from Sears, scalps
shaved to the quick in holy Mohawks,
who aim carnations at her and grin
like Happy Faces in *The Clockwork Orange,*

while signs posted on the pillars behind them
guarantee their First Amendment rights
and airport cops tell everyone
Keep Moving.

Eulene dodges tables
selling pictures of the Praying Hands.
She ducks into the women's lounge,
and bag ladies look up from the plastic chairs
as if she were already one of them.
When she double-checks her tickets,
the woman guard beside the hand dryer
demands to know whom she stole them from.

Why not? Eulene's passport
has been crammed since the day it was issued
with other people's travels.
How will she make it past
the check-in counter, the screening lines,
the Passengers Only Beyond This Point?

She's overshot the luggage limit,
her bags bulging with gadgets
her friends overseas could never
sneak past the customs clerks and drug-sniffing
dogs, and she hasn't even started
her own round of under-the-table errands.

The TSA matron runs her Geiger-counter
nightstick over her, and lets her go—
Eulene looks too much like
the mug-shot in her documents.
But when they wave her down the concourse,
the metal detection sirens go wild.
Her thoughts alone are confused enough
to fog the film in security cameras.

                                    Ah,
Eulene! With your lingering questions
and your great need to be shouted at,
your deepest feelings not yet crash-worthy—
how would you survive a year
in Mumbai, Delhi, or Kolkata?

DURGA-EULENE (THE MANY-ARMED)

I

Dejected by the latest screening
of her in-grown film, that mocking epic
Love 'Em and Get Lost,
Eulene decides enough's
enough. Time to put a layer
of Tuff-Kote on her soul.
Better yet, in this land
of juggernauts and thousand-headed gods,
to be reborn beyond all these turns
and twistings of the heart.

A light goes on in her brain
like a bare bulb in a godown.
She boards one of those overloaded
bashed-in double-decker death traps
that pass for public transport in this city.
She notes its number—*L* ("Hell") 9—
so she can tell someone in case
she doesn't come back in the body.

She jolts and lurches
through streets with bomb-crater potholes,
diesel fumes enveloping her
like a vengeful demiurge's wrath.
Her final stop Kumartali, the image-makers'
North Kolkata ghetto, to buy herself
her goddess get-up.

II

She picks out bangles, toe-rings,
the biggest nose-jewel she can keep
from sneezing at, a film star's
gaudy gold-streaked silks,
and a set of eight wooden
supernumerary arms
she hangs on her shoulder blades
like a dead-weight angel's wings . . .

Presto!

She's Durga the Terrible,
the Ten-Armed, with a coal-black fright wig
out of which snakes writhe, each hand
grasping discus or bow or flaming dart
the other deities donated as subscription
to the Destroyer-Goddess Fund.

(They sat in the splendor their Aryan-
warlord worshippers had imagined for them,
big-bellied *bons vivants,* nine-figure CEOs
on the board of the Puranic pantheon.
"A dame's the trick," they'd thundered,
"to do the cosmic mop-up.")
And Durga, good daughter, took up
the cudgel they'd issued her.

Not Eulene.
She brandishes her palm-fringe
fan to winnow weeds
from chaff: the deadbeats from the losers,
drifters and Don Juans, and those
who'd never join a club
that would admit them as a member.

She scrawls her latest motto
—মনে আর বসি্টস্—
in Bengali script so that no one
but a chosen few (who'd never
choose her anyway) can understand.
She mounts it on the lacey froth
of *shola* pith that fans out
like a peacock-tail of styrofoam
behind her.

                      She takes her trident-
headed spear to slay the demon Mahish—
image of everybody from her past
she'd like to do away with.

But Mahish is a clever con,
operating from a buffalo-skin cover
like the Mafia out of a church-front.
One of those dudes who's long gone
when the truth-spear skewers home
and spits the dumb-luck animal instead.

And Eulene's no avenging angel,
no theomorphic matador—
just a woman born of woman
with skin too pale for any latitude,
too thin for those who turn away
the minute they convince her to want them.

III
"What I want now,"
she thinks, staggering out
under her great weight of gew-gaws,

barking her towering tinsel tiara
against the Off-With-Their-Heads-
high bamboo struts of the thatch
and cardboard goddess shoppes,
"is a good stiff drink."

                              Stiff
as her fellow-goddesses, with their feet
(and arms and torsos) molded
from the same gray Hooghly River clay
unto which they will return
the day the chanting and garlanding
and sandalwood-paste adulation end.

Eulene walks away
to practice her one true discipline
and vanish into the throngs of worshippers
like an American into the suburbs.

IV
Fat chance. The cry goes up: *"It's SHE!!*
All hail!"

                         All hell breaks loose,
the crowd turns on her
for its theophanic thrill,
and the more Eulene protests
"I'm not your goddess!",
the more she flails her two true arms
and tries to beat a retreat
on her own two toe-ringed feet,
the more she gives the mob

what it's slavering for.
They hoist her into a rickshaw
above the crunch and splay and trample
of their passion, and pull her,
slowly and with ancient Sanskrit chantings,
to the river.

        Eulene looks on,
deity doll in the Festival of Cars,
thinking of Joan and Antoinette and Mary
Queen of Scots in their tumbrels.
Her fifty fingers clutch their token
tin-plate weaponry, effective as pop guns
trained on the Pentagon.
Her scattered mind finally points
one way: to the Meet-Your-Maker interface.

V
What, in the next few tickings
of the minute hand, can she make
her life worth? Not her name
in lights across some hardcore loner's
lovesick sky. Just
        herself,
her heart lost years ago
to solitude's harsh truths,
the break she could never force-fix
in this turn of the squeaky wheel.

No matter now.
The rickshaw on the stone steps
by the river, the crowd hefting her
on its shoulders, the Brahmin
in dingy *dhoti* and sacred thread

intoning the final *slokas*
before the reverential heave-ho . . .
. . . and Durga-Eulene sinks out of sight
to the bubbling of crocodiles' breath,
her final circle of admirers
closing in.

No *Hai Ram*
but a scrambled echo of Tagore
the last wavelength snaking
through her brain:

"Who knows
when Eulene's chains of fool's gold
will be off, and her soul's boat,
like the last glimmer of sunset,
vanish into the flotsam and jetsam
of this river filling up with night?"

for Paramita Banerjee

INTRALUDUS EULENEIAE

(Benares, 5 a. m.)

What now, Eulene? Your eyes blink open
on the dew-slick steps of the holy city,
mist drifting over the river before dawn
like the prehistoric musings of the Aryan gods.
What wisdom did you fathom
in the Ganges' sacred slime?
What knowledge or what powers put on
from the garlanded remains of sages
rowed out amidst the mournful chants
of their shaven-headed devotees
and dropped into mid-stream
from yellow cloths block-printed
with the names of God?

Not for you the harrowing of hell,
underwater halls of the afterworld.
Not for you the ash-smeared breast,
sandal-paste streaks on the forehead,
the matted hair and crazed eyes
of the Seers. Not for you the zero
at the center of the Sacred Word.

What goes under must rise again
say the apotheosophists, repeating
the sacrificial hero's thousand names,
giving the ancient story's prayer wheel
one more spin.

You, too,
have thrashed your way to the surface,
gasping for air in a language
not your own: its babble all around you
no more meaningless
than the trillion-year-old hum of galaxies
whirling in subatomic space.

Nothing to do but stand up,
still swaying like marsh grass
in the oily undulations slapping the steps
where you first clambered out.
Then stagger off, up dark medieval lanes
between cows and refugee vendors' stalls
and children begging among images
of the uncreated Lord—toward
something beyond either praise or blame.

Ready, at last, for anything.

EULENE AT KHAJURAHO

They're doing it all over the walls
of the Kandariya Mahadeo Temple
and Eulene's here by her lonesome.

The honeymoon couples come in droves,
pointing and giggling and holding furtive hands,
the girl's marriage vermilion
a blood-red question mark
down the parting of her hair.
When Eulene glances, envious, their way,
they jump apart like high-school paramours,
their sinning shamelessly unoriginal.

What else to do in a land
where sandstone lovers cavort and copulate
in high relief, and kissing is forbidden
in the films? At least they're better
than the prep-school boys from Delhi
or Bombay, whistling and ogling Eulene
and all her *firengi*-lady look-alikes,
howling "Hello, Madame!" as if they were
some *bustee's* hardcore layabouts, not the sons
of big industrialists with half their assets
in Swiss banks, the other half
the off-siphonings of Soviet aid.

The foreign tourists, with their Nikons,
their guidebooks in a dozen tongues,
and their easy-going sex lives,
are *blasé.* They've all slow-danced that way
—Shiva and his Shakti at the senior prom—
and in the parking lot above the bay,

they've watched the submarines race
from the back seat of his Chevy.

Eulene's hard up, though. Her donut,
at the moment, is all hole. She stares
at the friezes' venereal processionals
till their wind-pitted *Liebespaare*
are swimming in a blue-movie blur.

She wouldn't turn her nose up
at one of those round-cheeked, sloe-eyed,
dimple-chinned chaps in filmy wraparound
and shoulder-length earlobes, whipping up
a mag-wheel chariot with scimitars
for spokes, to teach her a thing or two
she can't get from the how-to books.

But she can't backdate her vital signs
a thousand years, and they can't unfasten
their lockstep from the stone.

                    What to do?
She slinks out of the compound—past
the tour guide in saffron and sacred ash
expounding on the four stages of life
she can't seem to get on with—into
the Nautch Girl Gift Emporium
("a Government Undertaking"), and tries
to bargain the boy shop-*wallah* down
from his ripped-off Kama Sutra price tag.
But at age ten he's been in
the tourist-skinning business
half his years, so she'll have to recall
what she skimmed while standing there.

She thinks of graying, dumpy men
lurking at newsstands in her country,
fondling copies of *Playboy,* hiding
their faces in the centerfolds.
Not one of them
who could stand on his hands
while doing it.

                Eulene needs a new lease
on her libido. Not on these temples
where erogenous zones are shackled
in some ritual re-enactment
of the Cosmic Oomph.

            For her
no surrogates or personals-ads applicants,
no fatted calves on the horned altars
of the lady-killer's art. No saints,
no clinging vines disguised as loners,
no would-be polygamists repeating themselves
from the days they were the know-it-all
generation.

              No one, in fine, who lives up
to what the chipped, eroded limbs of lovers
have struggled toward these thousand years—
stones resolving themselves slowly.
With great patience.

Into stone.

                      for Anne Monius

EULENE GOES BACK TO GODHEAD

Godhead or Bust, Eulene might have said once
but now she's not so sure,
doing the rounds with the shrouded walkers—
women from Newton Highlands or Palm Springs
muffled in saffron saris and sandal paste,
chanting the names of God a thousand times
to make their daily quota,
gliding in ankle-chained bare feet
across the temple's chilly, pigeon-dung-
encrusted floor till the sun's hauled up
from the horizon like a stolen butter churn.

Eulene knows her karma is to offend everyone
just once, so what is she doing here?
These women have come a long way, baby,
on their own credit cards, to go back
beneath the veil, do the Krishna-conscious
two-step, and peer out at the men
from behind the ladies' minimum-security screen.

Men in tunics and wrap-arounds
of streaked and faded orange,
heads shaved down to the follicles,
arms aloft in a victory symbol
drained of circulation,
bellowing their blissed brains out
as the finger cymbals stutter.

These dudes have turned the palm-leaf pages
all the way back to the *Vedas.*
In this ambience, Eulene and her entourage
—no matter their law degrees, their Lysistratic

vanguard, their vigilante litigators
in every state—are only what
they've always been:

                    Mere women,
figments of some minor demiurge's
overactive glands, male brains'
mirages who've had the audacity
to take on flesh and spend the entirety
of history distracting men.

So much for Germaine and Gloria and Title IX.
So much for Rosie the Riveter and the Hite Report.
Let them stay in the shadow
of the mud-walled huts: barefoot,
boiling the lentils to a brown-gray mush,
breeding a baby a year in a land
where only the cow is sacred.

The charred widows on the dead men's pyres
raise their blackened hands, brides
in glory in a kerosene-flame mandorla
cry out to them to save themselves
while they can.

                    Eulene's fellow-temptresses
prostrate themselves before the oil-
smudged lamps in doll's dress
that pass in these parts
as emanations of the cthonic gods.

What can Eulene do about it?
What's written in the stars crossed
on the palm lines can't be changed,
say the sages who splatter milk and butter

on the sacred fire. Which is interpreted,
It's all Eulene's fault for existing.

Eulene's path has always been the one
of most resistance, but now
if she can't join them, she'll beat them
at their own game—inviting the whole troupe out
for soya chips and curried yeast
at Govinda's "All-Veg" Bar and Grill,
signing the forms in triplicate
to spearhead a local chapter
of the Cow Protection League.

                              Still,
she can't believe anyone would go so ga-ga
over a blue-skinned, cow-eyed boy
who lolls around in filmy skirts, tinsel
tiaras, and fat flower *leis* like a tourist
at a *luau,* fingering a dime-store piccolo,
his Mona Lisa smirk so maddening
the bare-breasted village girls rip off
the remainder of their scanty threads
and fling themselves at his feet.
What Elvis had it better?

Eulene leafs through a technicolor-cover copy
of the *Gita* ("As It Is") for answers,
frowning at its wicked passions
and specious deaths, its questionable
translations and dubious interpretations.
She knows not what
she should be grateful for.

                                        Suddenly
a trumpet ought to sound offstage,
Eulene look up: Arjuna's chariot,
complete with fly-whisks and parasols
and scythe-blades on the wheels,
come swinging low for to carry her
out of here. No one since Medea
would have had it easier.

But that Being clutching the reins
with half-a-dozen of His countless hands,
His countless heads swiveling
in all directions—infinite of mouths and eyes,
infinite of bellies—standing in a car
that is no car, but Ezekiel's wheel's
Eastern counterpart, radiating
with the brilliance of a million suns:
the Voice out of the whirlwind,
the saint's brain blasted on Patmos . . .

. . . *This is the Face that no man sees*
and lives, Eulene thinks. Then,
Thank God that I'm a woman.

At that, the vision crumples
but Eulene is free, she's left off
all chanting and singing and telling
of beads, her earthly vehicle
having blooped straight through
to the Empyrean and back again.

Now she'll go on chopping wood
and carrying water—the bland
fanatic wisdom of her daily round.

                                        for Rebecca Manring

EULENE MEETS CROW / EULENE EATS CROW

I
Out of the estuarine crocodile's snaggled jaws,
out of the mud-colored snort
of the wild boar, browsing hock-
         deep in primordial slime,
out of the deadly chiaroscuro of sunlight
in thickets where the Bengal tiger blinks
and whole subspecies of foliage rearrange themselves
like silks around the throne of a potentate,
out of the miasma, the stunted
saline verdure of the Sunderbans,
stunned and sun-weary, flapped

Crow

that brackish-billed anathema,
on a weekend tour of the desperate delta's
last paradisiacal standoff,
in a private launch doing loops through channels
where hand-adzed atavistic scows
groaned to their gunnels
with teak, mahogany, and pearls--
all the unprotected renderings of a preserve
the government has set aside for spoilage.

Where boatmen poled their slow-motion plunder
upstream to the nearest port,
and sang ballads in mournful modes
about honey-gatherers scraped up limb-
by-limb between the hives
after some stiff-jointed, superannuated man-eater
limped out of cover and sampled them
for the sweetness of their flesh.

Neither off-course nor off his feed,
Crow relished these legends of gore
and groanings wrested from the throat.
New additions to his repertoire.
He squawked and hopped up and down on the top
of his Port-a-Parrot carrier,
straining at his thin tin shackle
till it snapped . . .

       . . . while his master, crouching at the prow
and peering through binoculars,
chatted with the *aides-de-camp*
and took notes on shadows flitting behind
the green *purdah*-curtain of the forest.

Ignored, Crow
spied his chances,
soared remorselessly off.

II
Meanwhile, upriver
in her ancestral watering-hole,
Kukurpukur, her Dogpatch-on-the-Delta—

Eulene.

Begum Eulene, with teased and hennaed beehive
and Mandarin-lacquered claws,
swathed in some filmy, glitter-sprinkled thing
that revealed more than it concealed
but veiled her up to the eyelids. Begum
Eulene, practiced in all the arts of entrapment,
with eunuchs to do her dirty work.

She was plotting her escape to the capital,
away from this down-country duchess's
idler's life: nothing to do
but supervise the cook's boy
whacking at cabbages with a king-sized scimitar,
squabble with the sultan's wives
and listen through the lattice-work grille
of the women's wing to the hum
of the rice crop growing. Might as well
be Dubuque as Daulatpur.

She put on her see-through *burkha*.
With her favorite eunuch, Iqbal
"Sneaky" Siddiqi, she crept out
through the cistern window, dropped
like a black leaf to the road below
and hailed the nearest rickshaw into town.

Now she lounged under the rotting canvas canopy
of Hussein's Tea Stall and Kebab-O-Rama,
swatting at flies and smoldering in the sultry air
like some Thirties' cinema spitfire,
looking to the local oglers like a *houri*
from Hell.

III
Suddenly, out of the sun
blasting its jackhammer
through every shanty off the square,
exploded Crow.

What had he noticed below?
Tinfoil fringes shimmering on the handlebars
of rickshaws, bottle shards glinting
in trash outside the tea stalls?

Crow's belly rumbled,
thunder in a blackening sky.
Words like "Truth" and "Beauty"
corkscrewed through his brain, his appetite
dangerously close to melt-down.

He closed his wings and dropped
to a heap of used banana plates
glorified with a nimbus of fruit flies . . .

as Eulene whipped her seed-pearl veil
back over her face and stepped out
into mid-day's purgatorial blaze.

She met Crow
at the nadir of his dive-
bomb: a black hole colliding
with a neutron star.

They picked themselves up
and stared each other down—the recognition
instant: two zeros canceling each other out.

Crow unruffled his feathers and preened
his pinions, a perfect study in nonchalance.
Eulene, too, could do indifference
but for this show she hunched her hackles
and raised her *burkha's* anthracite-mesh wings—
the pose crows know as Raven-Feigns-Rage.

Could they gabble to each other, and from
their colloquy across the species
cobble together a world? Not in this
stunned din, as the negative force fields fused
and all Kukurpukur imploded . . .

They'd tried their best to satisfy
the catastrophists, as the earth collapsed into random
gas and protoplasmic goo.

Eulene and Crow flapped off into the phlogiston
past the last tatter of the ozone layer.

The planet gone *poof* beneath them.

for Ted Hughes and the original Crow

EULENE DECLARES

I am not a woman
    I am a force of nature

I am not a thundercloud or a cloudwall
    I am a burst of incoming fire

I am not a fire base
    I am a tangle of Himalayan blackberries
covering the headland

I am not a dark plot to disentangle in the novel's
    final chapter
        I am the last task crossed off the list
on your night stand

I am not the constellation of Cygnus or
    the Cruz del Sur
        I am the cry of geese migrating by the
wintry glow of cell towers

I am not the light of your life
    I am the echo of generations painted
on cave walls

I am not the mirror or the lamp
    I am the first gleam along the continent's
serrated blade

I am not the exile's transcontinental flight
    I am a crystal chip swirling for years into the
blue-green torment of glacial melt

I am not the natural child of silence and slow time
    I am the lost offspring of a tilting shelf,
  a miscellany of obstreperous bells

I am not a whim of weather or the vicissitudes of birth
    I am a woman straight and strong

I am not a force of nature
    I am a woman

for Eugenia Toledo

NOTES ON THE POEMS

"Mania Klepto"

The premise comes from a Jerry Lewis joke Eulene heard once as she walked past a television set in her childhood—what if someone felt compelled to go into stores and put things there instead of shoplifting?

Success Bomb #45

Long before the word "terrorist" had become a verbal weapon of mass destruction, post-9/11, Eulene had been calling herself a "success terrorist," as tribute to her skill in undermining all her efforts to get ahead. She had scrawled out pages of notes in journals and on scratch paper about this unique skill set of hers, but nothing had quite coalesced. After 9/11, though, a series of layoffs from her own—and several other people's—jobs compelled Eulene to take a break from her Sisyphean schedule and pamper herself in a bubble bath, while browsing through John Berryman's *Dream Songs*. Eulene's search for wisdom (and career tips) in this Song of Songs for self-saboteurs caused her to take a second look at both her prospects and her prosody. The result was a "poetic palimpsest": Eulene's scattered Confessions compressed into an 18-line, three-sestet, slant-rhyming homage to the Berryman form, particularly the infamous "Dream Song #45." By then, the word "bomb" had gained new and provocative resonances, so it supplanted the overly, ahem, explosive "terrorist."

On a more pragmatic note, Eulene wonders about the repercussions of reading an e-book in the bath, and her chances of survival if she accidentally dropped it in the water. Would she be electrocuted, stewed in her own skin-pampering solutions? Or would the e-book merely be ruined, and cost her a cool K or so to replace? On the other hand, if Eulene dropped one of those old-fangled paper editions into the bath, a new used copy could be acquired at any local bookstore for a dozen dollars or so. With such a frugal purchase, though, she would not be doing enough to stimulate the economy: the GDP might, uh, bomb. Ruin truly would stare back—but by then, Eulene would be meeting Berryman's Henry on the other, smoking shore . . .

Woman, Money, Watch, Gun

Some years ago, poet Lisel Mueller gave an exercise at the Port Townsend Writers' Conference—to begin a poem with the lines, "He wakes with a start. / Something missing: woman, / money, watch, gun." These turned out to be the opening lines of "Doing Hard Time," by Margaret Haase, from her book *Stars Above, Stars Below* (New Rivers Press, 1989). Eulene's irreverent and irrelevant response to Haase's poem was later published in *Ploughshares,* and recorded for the magazine's "Dial-a-Poem" service. Eulene, of course, jammed the phone lines that entire week, ringing up Dial-a-Poem over and over to hear her exploits given such exposure by so prominent a literary magazine. Could this be why *Ploughshares* later discontinued Dial-a-Poem?

"Step on Your Watch" has been recorded by the JB Horns, with Pee Wee Ellis, Maceo Parker, and Fred Wesley. Eulene used to dance to it in a teeny-bopper daze.

Durga-Eulene

The phrase in Bengali script in part II is transliterated English—"men are beasts"—one of Eulene's many befogged and self-evidently contradictory notions about the male species.

"Hai Ram" ("Oh God" or literally "Oh Rama") were Mahatma Gandhi's last words after he was shot by an assassin on January 30, 1948. Many Hindus believe that to call out to God as their last utterance will ease the soul's transition to the next life.

Intraludus Euleneiae

In the sacred city of Benares (Varanasi) the bank of the Ganges River is lined with some of India's most ancient Hindu temples. The *ghats,* the steps leading down to the river from the temples, are used for cremation of dead Hindu faithful, many of whom travel to Benares in the last days of their lives so as to be able to die in one of Hinduism's most holy places. Although most Hindus practice cremation of their dead, the bodies of some priests and infants are simply wrapped in *namāboli* (cloth printed with prayers) and lowered into the river.

Eulene Meets Crow/Eulene Eats Crow

Ted Hughes was Guest of Honor at the Second—and last—Asia Poetry Festival held in Dhaka, Bangladesh, in November 1989, a fête hosted by Bangladesh's then-President H. M. Ershad. One of Mr. Hughes's chief interests in accepting Ershad's invitation to Bangladesh was to visit the Sunderban, the forest covering the delta region of the Ganges River. It is one of the last remaining wild preserves of the Royal Bengal Tiger, which Mr. Hughes hoped to see in its natural habitat.

Meanwhile, Eulene had recently arrived in the guise of personal factotum and gadfly-in-waiting to an American poet and translator (a.k.a. *moi*). Unable to languish indefinitely in the luggage storage area of this poet's Dhaka lodgings, Eulene burst out and found herself in surreptitious attendance at the poetry festival, seeking Crow (who had also not been invited.) There, unaware of Eulene's (and Crow's) shadow-presences, the American poet met Hughes and learned of his plan to see the Sunderban during his stay in Bangladesh.

After Mr. Hughes's return to England, the poem began to struggle forth from the creative primal ooze, after Eulene stowed aboard the launch bearing the American poet on her own visit to the Sunderban. Mr. Hughes was in fact amused when Eulene informed him that she had plotted such a meeting with his poetic character since she had first read *The Life and Songs of the Crow* back in graduate school. She had bided her time, merely waiting for her occasion.

An early version of this poem, which Eulene sent to Crow in England a few months later, is among Ted Hughes's papers in the Special Collections Department of Emory University's Robert F. Woodruff Library. The American poet was moved to see this and other correspondence when she was permitted to view these papers a few weeks after Ted Hughes's death.

DISQUIETING MUSE: THE "EULENE" SERIES

Eulene's utterly contrived generation, and mystifying (if not stupefying) birth took place sometime in the fall of my first semester as a student of the Creative Writing program at Syracuse University. At first this nascent shadow-figure was nameless, amorphous: a source of unease and guilty displeasure who kept cropping up in otherwise well-behaved poetic exercises. This character—"my double" or "my shadow," as my scribblings lamely titled her—took over the outpourings of my night sweats, and began to co-opt my moments of lucid-insomniac inspiration, muddled and non-Borgian as they were. She shoved me away from my grad-student work station and began to wreak havoc upon the speakers in the "serious, well-made," New Criticism-influenced poems I was trying to compose at the time. She seemed determined to function as a sort of Doppelganger-cum-Dr. Jekyll / Ms. Hyde figure upon whom I could project emotions I dared not attribute to myself as a responsible member of the body politico-poetic. That was fine, as long as she was prepared to take the blame . . . and to pick up the tab for any lawsuits.

But soon she demanded a name: the most irksome, clingy, oleaginous name I could summon up from the wellsprings of memory—Eulene—the moniker of a high-school drama coach whom I had adored and feared at the time, and who had been one of my first mentors among strong-minded, self-directed professional women in the arts. Eulene Reed will forgive me, I hope, for misappropriating her unusual and memorable given name for such poetic irreverences.

Along with a name, of course, came a separate and distinct identity: like characters in novels, Eulene assumed a life of her own. She insisted on her place in the world, much as natural forces compel an infant to be released from the womb at the end of its term. In effect, Eulene, self-created, chose *moi* as her vatic instrument, her reluctant mouthpiece; and she heaped coals of fire upon my tongue if I, the serious student of Creative Writing, attempted to evade or elude her dae-mon. For further indoctrination, Eulene directed her poetic lackey to read, not the poetry of high seriousness and elegiac regret, but "Howl" and "Naked Lunch" and other works of Beat extravagance. The young poet's colleagues and fellow graduate students suggested further literary excesses such as "The Dream Songs" by John Berryman and Ted Hughes's "Crow."

The first dozen of Eulene's misadventures blighted my po-etic life during the fall and winter months of my first year in the Creative Writing program, and were yoked violent-ly to the otherwise bland and well-behaved manuscript of the Thesis in Poetry. But Eulene had not yet finished having her way with me, and after a long period of quiescence, she re-emerged full-blown, right where she had left off, in the se-ries of absurdities beginning with "Eulene's *Noche Oscura*." Since then, she has dragged me hither and thither about the planet, compelling me to indulge in subaltern post-structur-alist (dis)courses and engage in acts of lurid anomaly that violate socio-poetic norms. She stowed away in my baggage when I departed for Kolkata on fellowship, and demanded a full-fare ticket to accompany me to Bangladesh (I had to sit in luggage-compartment steerage, with the port-a-pet carri-ers). She took on the Developing World, and I could only stand by in fascinated horror as she carried out her schemes to topple Developed World preconceptions as if these were governments.

She now demands that I take courses in the Old Testament jeremiad and Elizabethan invective, bureaucratic baffle-gab and cybernetic compu-speak, in preparation for what looms ominously on the horizon: the ever-widening, techno-trash-littered on-ramp to the information superhighway. If either of us is to be a casualty of the downsized, outsourced, post-industrial, post-employment, health benefits-free, si-multaneously globalized and balkanized, leaner and meaner Brave New Sweatshop, it will certainly not be Eulene. Her world-consternating exploits threaten to run beyond book-length, and there is no end in sight.

ACKNOWLEDGMENTS

Grateful acknowledgment is made to the following periodicals in which many of these poems, some in earlier versions, first appeared:

Artful Dodge, Bellingham Review, The Cincinnati Review, Colorado-North Review, Colorado Review, Disquieted Muses Quarterly, Ekleksographia, International Quarterly, The Iowa Review, Jeopardy, Lady Jane's Miscellany, Malahat Review, Mangrove, Margie, Michigan Quarterly Review, Montana Review, New Letters, North American Review, Ploughshares, Poetry Northwest, The Smith, Venture, Whiskey Island, Willow Springs, Wisconsin Review, Writers Forum.

A few of these poems appeared in *Premonitions of an Uneasy Guest* (Hardin-Simmons UP, 1983; Limited edition).

Several of these poems appeared in a limited edition, privately printed chapbook, *Brief Irreveries* (Maryland Institute College of Art, 1997) with graphics by Allegra Marquart.

"Intraludus Euleneiae" (as "Eulene Between Acts") was reprinted in the anthology *Knowing Stones: Poems of Exotic Places,* ed. Maureen Tolman Flannery (John Gordon Burke, 2000.)

"Eulene" and "Woman, Money, Watch, Gun" were reprinted in the chapbook *Carolyne Wright: Greatest Hits 1975 - 2001,* Pudding House Publications, 2002.

Thanks to the Mary Ingraham Bunting Institute of Radcliffe College; the Council for International Exchange of Scholars; the Centrum Foundation; the New York State Council for the Arts; the Fine Arts Work Center in Provincetown; the Indo-U. S. Subcommission on Education and Culture; the Maryland Institute College of Art; the National Endowment for the Humanities, and Partners of the Americas; the Creative Writing Programs of Cleveland State University, the University of Miami, and Syracuse University; and the Virginia Center for the Creative Arts for awards, fellowships, and other practical support while I was writing the poems in this book.

For their reading of and suggestions for poems in this manuscript while it was in progress, I am grateful to Tom Aslin, Marvin Bell, the Milton Center Workshop, Jim Daniels, Madeline DeFrees, Stephanie Painter, Jim Parrott, W. D. Snodgrass, and especially Deborah Woodard. Thanks also to editors Sally Ashton, Don Bogen, Dan Bourne, Pamela Gemin, Laurence Goldstein, Vince Gotera, David Hamilton, DeWitt Henry, James McKinley, Robert Nazarene, William O'Daly, Joyce Peseroff, Judith Skillman, Robert Stewart, and David Wagoner for their interest in this work. And major thanks to Eugenia Toledo for creating Eulene, in her own image, for the cover.

ABOUT THE POET

CAROLYNE WRIGHT has published nine books and chapbooks of poetry; four volumes of poetry translated from Spanish and Bengali, including the anthology, *Majestic Nights: Love Poems of Bengali Women* (White Pine Press, 2008); and a volume of essays. Her most recent collection, *A Change of Maps* (Lost Horse Press, 2006), finalist for the Idaho Prize and Alice Fay di Castagnola Award of the Poetry Society of America, won the 2007 IPPY Bronze Award. Her previous book, *Seasons of Mangoes and Brainfire* (Carnegie Mellon University Press/EWUP Books, second edition 2005), received the Blue Lynx Prize and American Book Award. A poem of hers appeared in *The Best American Poetry 2009* and in the *Pushcart Prize XXXIV: Best of the Small Presses* (2010). She is a Contributing Editor for the Pushcart Prizes. Wright served on the Board of Directors of the Association of Writers and Writing Programs (AWP) for 2004-2008, and has taught at universities, colleges, and writers' conferences throughout the U. S. In 2005 she returned to her native Seattle, where she is on the faculty of the Northwest Institute of Literary Arts' Whidbey Writers Workshop MFA Program.

CPSIA information can be obtained at www.ICGtesting.com
Printed in the USA
266151BV00001B/1/P